This Christmas Coloring Book
Belongs To:

____

____

Write and Draw to Express Yourself

Date: ___ / ___ / ___

Date: ___/___/___

Write and Draw to Express Yourself

Date: ___/___/___

Write and Draw to Express Yourself

Date: ___ / ___ /

Date: _______/_____/_____

Write and Draw to Express Yourself

Date:

Write and Draw to Express Yourself

Date: _______ / /

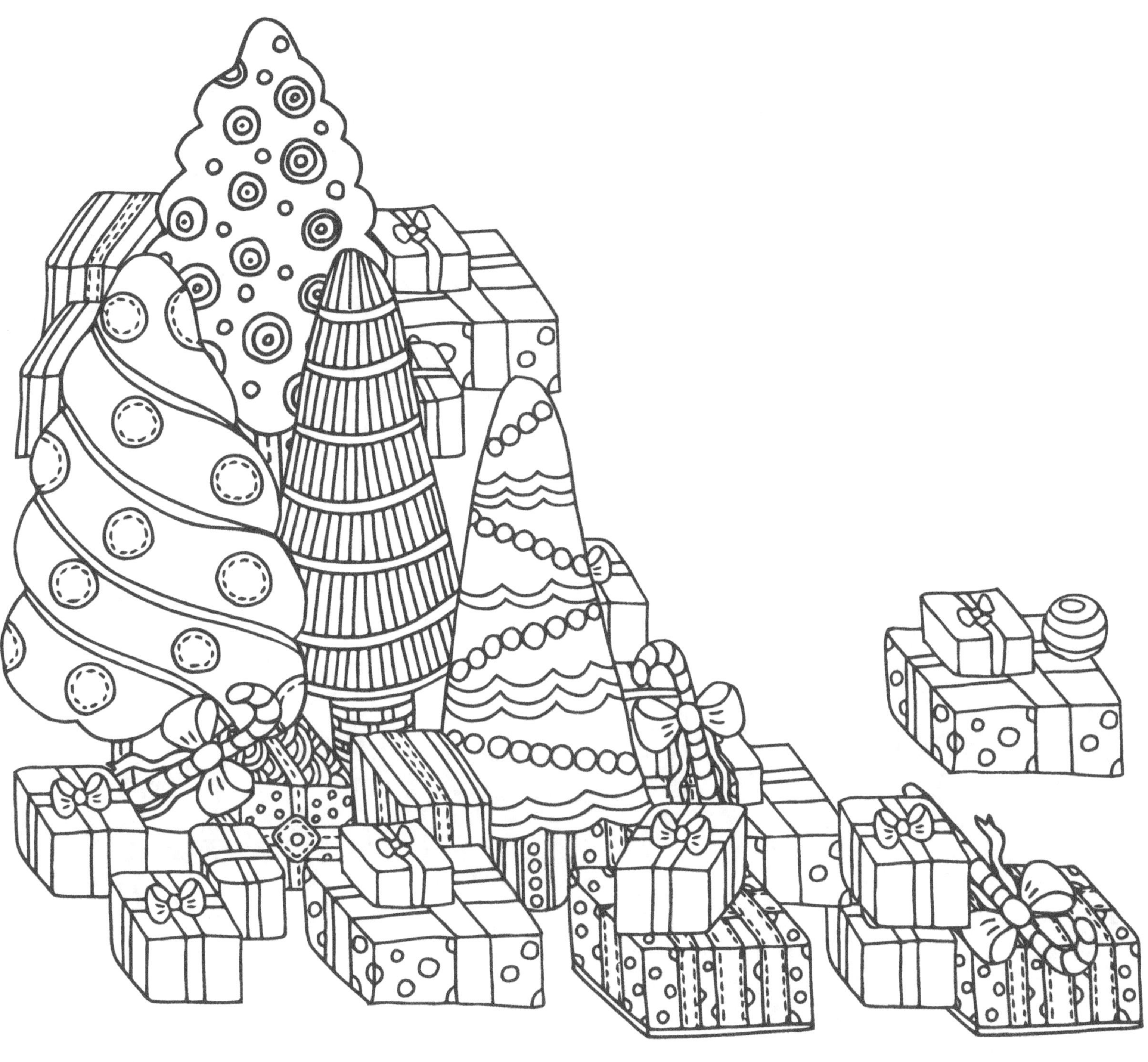

Date: ___ / ___ / ___

Write and Draw to Express Yourself

Date: ___/___/___

Write and Draw to Express Yourself

Date: ___/___/___

Date: _____ / ___ / ___

Write and Draw to Express Yourself

Date:
xmas

Write and Draw to Express Yourself

Date:

Write and Draw to Express Yourself

Date:

Write and Draw to Express Yourself

Date: ___ / ___ / ___

Christmas
Time

Write and Draw to Express Yourself

Date: _____ / __ / __

Write and Draw to Express Yourself

Date: _____ / ___ / ___

Write and Draw to Express Yourself

Date: ___/___/___

Date: ___/___/___

Write and Draw to Express Yourself

Date: ___ / ___ / ___

Merry Christmas

Write and Draw to Express Yourself

Date: ___/___/___

Write and Draw to Express Yourself

Date: ___/___/___

Write and Draw to Express Yourself

Date: ___/___/___

Write and Draw to Express Yourself

Date: ___/___/___

Write and Draw to Express Yourself

Date:

Write and Draw to Express Yourself

Date: _____ / ___ / ___

Write and Draw to Express Yourself

Write and Draw to Express Yourself

Date: ___ / ___ / ___

Write and Draw to Express Yourself

The
Magic of
Christmas

Write and Draw to Express Yourself

Write and Draw to Express Yourself

Date:

Date: _______ / ___ / ___

Write and Draw to Express Yourself

Write and Draw to Express Yourself

Date: ___/___/___

Date: ___/___/___

Write and Draw to Express Yourself

Date:

Write and Draw to Express Yourself

Date: ___/___/___

Write and Draw to Express Yourself

Write and Draw to Express Yourself

Write and Draw to Express Yourself

peace
&
joy

Write and Draw to Express Yourself

Date: _______ / ___ / ___

Date: ___/___/___

Write and Draw to Express Yourself

Date: ___ / ___ / ___

Write and Draw to Express Yourself

Date:

Write and Draw to Express Yourself

Write and Draw to Express Yourself

Date: ___/___/___

Date: _____ / ____ / ______

Date: _____/___/_____

Write and Draw to Express Yourself

Date: _____ / ___ / _____

Write and Draw to Express Yourself

Date: